SALFORD IN PICTURES

Greengate from the Irwell, 1973.

SALFORD
IN PICTURES

an outline of the growth of an industrial town

by V. I. TOMLINSON

E. J. MORTEN (Publishers)
Didsbury, Manchester, England

Published 1974
E. J. MORTEN (Publishers)
Warburton Street, Didsbury,
Manchester, England.

ISBN 0 901598 49 6/1973

Printed and Bound in Great Britain by
THE SCOLAR PRESS LIMITED,
59/61 East Parade, Ilkley, Yorkshire.

INTRODUCTION

Recent press notices widely publicised that, in 1844, Friedrich Engels called Salford *the* 'classic slum'. Engels did not use this phrase. Although he presented a grim picture of Salford slums he used twenty times as many words to be equally scathing about the more extensive slum areas of neighbouring Manchester. Indeed, with other writers, he described the evils of the slums in Birmingham and Nottingham and Leeds and London in similar vein while recent remnants of such districts, in most large towns, confirm that there was very little difference between them. This ubiquity was recognised by Engels when he averred that 'every great city has one or more slums' which 'are pretty equally arranged in all the great towns in England'. Nearly all were a legacy of the rapid and planless urban expansion associated with industrial growth when economic factors, technical considerations and profit motives governed development. As devised, the buildings which resulted frequently provided an improvement on previous conditions. Both domestic and industrial slums often stemmed from misuse or inertia associated with the slowness with which the fabric of a town changed in response to new ideas and new techniques. These were usually translated in the nineteenth century into structures on virgin land and this peripheral growth and central decay, which was characteristic of the period, was also appreciated by Engels. Fifty years after his original comments on the slums of Salford and Manchester, he wrote that 'the most crying abuses have either disappeared or have been made less conspicuous. But what of that? Whole districts which in 1844 I could describe as almost idyllic have now, with the growth of the towns, fallen into the same state of delapidation, discomfort and misery'. In comparing the new with the old slums, he went on to say that 'only the pigs and the heaps of refuse are no longer tolerated', but they were still close by for, over ten years after his death, Salford Council was asked to declare thirteen styes in Irwell Street, off residential Whit Lane, to be unfit on sanitary grounds—for the keeping of swine.

It is true that the worst housing evils in Salford were gradually eliminated many years ago but the rate of clearance of later property, which has now become sub-standard, has been accelerated. Post-war government action and private property development schemes, as in nearly all English towns, mean that extensive residential areas and obsolete industrial buildings are being swept away and their sites re-developed. At the same time, boundary commission recommendations are being implemented and it is therefore an appropriate time to record changes in a city which illustrates, within 5,200 acres, most of the typical aspects of what might aptly be termed a classic industrial town. Engels would probably have accepted this phrase equally with his statement that 'Manchester is the classic type of a modern manufacturing town' but the task of outlining the inter-relation of industry and housing is simplified in Salford because of its relative compactness.

A first survey of the growth of Salford should preferably be in pictures so that it is unfortunate that limitations of space compel the size of the illustrations to be curtailed. As it is also desirable that as many different aspects as possible should be depicted their reduced size does permit the reproduction of 280 illustrations in the seventy pages which are available.

Commonplace twentieth century street nameplates are frequently introduced as a reminder that everyday names can preserve links with Salford's industrial growth in the nineteenth century or its medieval history or even its earlier days, over a thousand years ago. In the present period of rapid change, when vast areas are being altered, names of contemporary significance are often given to new 'courts', 'houses', 'ways', 'gardens' or streets but it is to be hoped that as many of the old names as possible will be perpetuated to maintain this thread of history.

Although placenames may be the commonest link with the past, the present visual outline is more concerned with material things and stresses the changing face of the townscape. It is an incomplete picture, however, because it deals only with homes and industries. The part played by individual Salfordians in the city's development is not included. This is regrettable for a city lives because of the spirit of its people; yet, again, space does not allow consideration of the spiritual, cultural and recreational associations which this has fostered or the churches, schools, theatres, clubs and pubs which have then been created to lend diversity to the houses and workshops which are illustrated in the following pages.

Salford.
August 1973.

7

BEGINNINGS

Twenty acres of Salford may have seen little change for 2000 years. The paths across them have become more sunken (1) and coarser grasses have begun to intrude on the moorland vegetation but Kersal Moor still looks like other uplands in south Lancashire where early man dwelt, outside the densely wooded and marshy areas. As on similar sites, he left behind stone tools and weapons and some evidence of a small flint factory was found in 1886, while the 1908 discovery of a stone spindle whorl (2) indicates early textile manufacture. A mace head (3) found at Mode Wheel in 1890, possibly carried there by the river, a burial urn excavated from a mound in Broughton Park in 1873 and a bronze axehead (5), said to be from the same area, show continuity of occupation. Simple hut dwellings (8) were the usual form of shelter in this type of environment.

Manchester and two roads passed through Salford. That to Coccium (probably at Wigan), crossed the Irwell by a ford at Ordsall, followed the line of Hodge Lane and left traces of its course in Pendleton fields, as shown on the

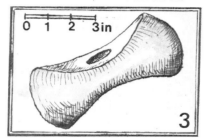

8   The Romans established a fort at

1848 map of the area west of Hope Hall (10). The road to Ribchester followed the route of Bury New Road, was excavated further north (7) and left twentieth century legacies in the narrow street behind the houses fronting the main road (9), a centurion's ring found on the site of St. John's Church Institute in 1912, and Roman coins from the adjacent Rectory grounds. A spurious modern link is at Ordsall (4) where the antiquary Barritt (1743-1820) gave a name to the Roman ford and postulated Christian occupation of a nearby heathen site which he called Woden's Cave (6).

From earliest times, the river would be used for transport through difficult terrain and the dug-out canoes occasionally found during excavations, as for the Ship Canal (11), usually date from about a thousand years ago.

FIRST WRITTEN RECORDS

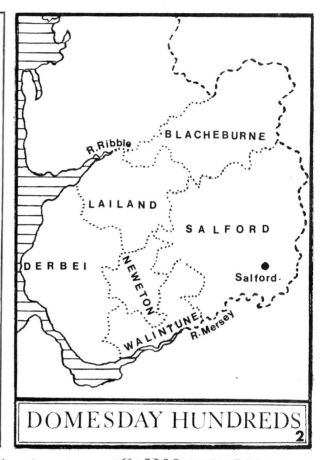

DOMESDAY HUNDREDS

When the Domesday survey (1) was made for William the Conqueror, in 1086, Salford was already of local importance for it had given its name to the surrounding district or 'hundred' (2), which continued with unchanged boundaries and name when the County of Lancaster was created. The town's standing in Saxon times was also suggested by the first sentence which records that 'King Edward (the Confessor) held Salford' but the rest of the entry presents a picture of a sparsely populated area.

About 1230, Randle de Blundeville, sixth earl of Chester, granted a charter to the town (9) which laid down a system under which it was governed for over 500 years. Enrolled burgesses could each have a burgage of one acre for which they had to pay twelve pence a year and this carried free pasture in the woods and on the plain. They also had commercial advantages for shoemakers, skinners, fullers and other craftsmen were protected from outside competitors. The seal depicts a feudal knight (3) whose shield shows that the city's armorial bearings, granted in 1844, provide a modern link with the Norman period for they bear the three gold wheatsheaves on a blue ground, as carried by the Earldom of Chester. These arms may be seen in diverse places in various media: stamped on official papers (5), carved in stone on the former customs house (4), set in mosaic at the entrance to the town hall, carved in wood in the Magistrates' Court (10), modelled in plaster in the Manchester Crown Court, cast in iron on some of the Irwell bridges (6), painted on many surfaces, engraved on civic glassware, fired into pottery for J. Hendry Boyd of Regent Road (7),

brilliantly worked out in flowers by the Parks Department for special occasions, printed on cloth to celebrate Edward VII's coronation (8) and embossed on old books in the city library.

Domesday Book gives the name *Salford* (1) but in a Pipe Roll of 1169 it is *Sauford*, in an Inquest of 1226 it is *Sainford*, in one of 1257 *Saltford*, in an Assize Roll of 1253 *de Selford* while *Shelford* was another early variation.

5

6

7

8

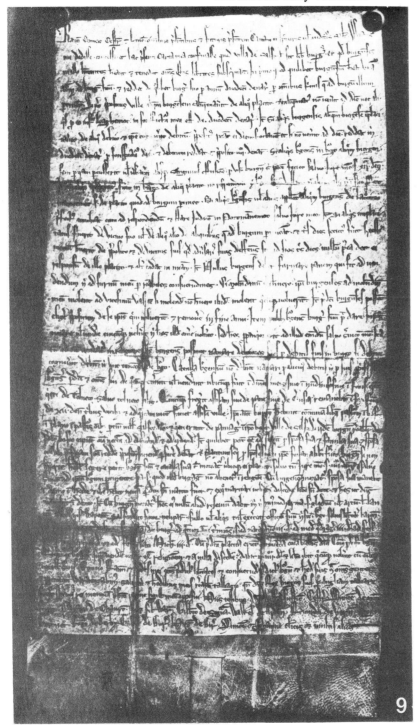

9

10

11

RURAL BACKGROUND

Nearly six hundred years after Salford received its charter, when Manchester and Salford began to develop as factory towns, it became popular to publish views of the urban centre as seen from the rural outskirts. Most of these were taken from places in Salford where the rising ground has always presented excellent vantage points for panoramas of the town centres.

Early nineteenth century engravings show that, even then, the major part of Salford was unspoilt countryside with the built-up area thinning out at Broughton Bridge and the Crescent. This open country was not all settled farmland and a few relics of the original landscape still remained. The flood plain of the Irwell was occupied by natural water meadows, the steep sides of the river and stream valleys were covered with virgin woodland and the higher land merged into Swinton Moor at Irlams-o'th-Height and Kersal Moor on the opposite side of the Irwell.

The outlook from Kersal in 1795 (1) changed very slowly and it is still possible to find vistas there with a rural foreground (4). One of the factors which opened up development in south Salford was the Regent Road tollbridge, shown in the view from Ordsall in 1824 (2). For about a further fifty years, the man in the foreground would have been able to walk his dog along a country lane, over fields and through Ordsall Wood to the unrestored fifteenth century hall. The Manchester, Bolton and Bury Canal was cut along the side of the Irwell valley from 1792 and, twenty-five years later, the towpath at the significantly named Strawberry Hill, Pendleton, offered a pleasant rural walk (3).

Bluebells were gathered in the woods at Weaste (5) in the nineteen twenties and in the Broughton cloughs and woodlands, shown in 1936 (4), bluebells and foxgloves still flourish, rabbits and hares are not uncommon and wild geese pass overhead each year.

12

Most of the large timber was commercially exploited in the nineteenth century (7) but remaining trees are now being made the subject of preservation orders (8, 9) so that present-day Salford retains some link with its country origin—in addition to Paradise, Blossom Street, Springfield Lane, Sandywell, Posey Row and similar byways (6) around downtown Greengate!

Conditions for Sale by Ticket At the House of James Leicester, the Running Horses, on Kersal Moor within Broughton in the County of Lancaster on Monday the third day of May 1819 at 3 o'clock in the afternoon of

Lot 2. 50 Oaks from N.º 51 to 100 inclusive now growing on Estates in Broughton and Kersall belonging to the Reverend John Clowes.

Number On Map	Description	Situa
T5	Sycamore	15 Ma
T6	Sycamore	5 St.
T7	Lime	3 St.
T8	Sycamore	475 B
G6	9 Lime, 3 Hawthorn, 16 Sycamore, 3 Elm, 1 Chestnut, 3 Holly	471 B Moor rear. Elect Paul'
G7	3 Chestnut, 6 Ash,	The B

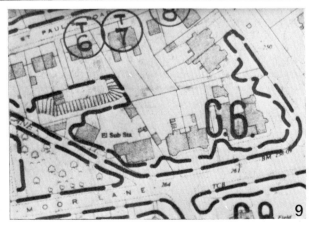

MANORS

Clearing the woodlands and bringing the waste lands into cultivation would largely be undertaken by the holders of the medieval manors and larger estates.

Ordsall Hall (1), renovated and re-opened in 1972, recalls the scale of buildings for a manor house with a reminder of feudal organisation in its important great hall. In particular, the story of its tenure by the Radcliffes shows the influence of early land-owning families. Broughton Hall (3) was held—and mortgaged—by relatives of the Earls of Derby before passing to the Clowes family and the remaining records of the manor court again reveal something of the persistence of this influence into the eighteenth century. Even the present-day purchaser of a house on former Clowes land may find a reminder of manorial days in his deeds (6). Kersal Hall and Kersal

3

4

5

Cell (2) were important half-timbered houses with estates in the Irwell valley while, on the opposite side of the river, Pendleton Old Hall occupants (5) improved land which became more valuable for its water and mineral rights.

By contrast with the older houses, Hope Hall (4) showed the graciousness of a Georgian structure for, shortly after 1750, the medieval building had been completely rebuilt in the current fashion by Daniel Bayley. It had further sympathetic additions before its demolition, about 1956. T. B. Bayley, who died in 1803, provides a classic example (as chairman of the magistrates; high sheriff from the age of 24, F.R.S., colonel in the Volunteers, President of the local Board of Health, encourager of agricultural experiments, disciple of John Howard, anti-slavery worker and holder of other offices) of the continuing influence of the land-owning families up to the changing society at the beginning of the nineteenth century.

To hold the same with the appurts (subject to the performance of the usual and accustomed suit and service at the Court Baron of the Manor of Broughton —) unto the said Purchaser and his exs heirs.

6

TUDOR TOWN

By about 1650 when the first map of Salford was produced (6) the small town in the bend of the Irwell, with its timber framed buildings as on Serjeant Street (4), was a smaller version of today's 'Tudor' tourist centres at Chester or Ludlow or Lavenham. The last of these black and white buildings to be demolished, after its closure in 1931, was the 'Bull's Head' (2), an old tavern occupying the town house of the Allen family and showing the ancient 'cruck' method of construction (3).

4

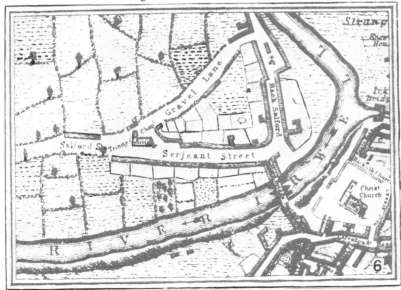

5

Salford Bridge (1), which preceded the present Victoria Bridge, was on the site of the old ford from which the town took its name and was the only link with Manchester. As was common, the houses clustered round a market place and cross (7) with the stocks and courthouse nearby. Here, local government was centred in the meetings of the court leet. Salford museum preserves the portmote records (5) which give a lively picture of the Tudor town with its thatched roofs and daub walls, its street 'mydinges', blocked water courses and primitive roads. Although some craftsmen are mentioned, occupations were generally linked with some work on the land.

6

7

HUMPHREY BOOTH

Although the introduction stated that there would be no attempt to deal with people who had played important roles in Salford's history, it is difficult to consider its changing face without mention of Humphrey Booth. His gravestone (2), which records that he died in 1635, is now, appropriately, inside Sacred Trinity Church after being found, face downwards, in Manchester Cathedral in 1894. The family residence was Booth Hall (1), off Greengate, and Humphrey built and endowed Sacred Trinity, the first church in Salford (5), which was consecrated in the year of his death.

A charity, carefully planned to aid 'poor, aged, needy or impotent' residents of his native town, was created by the allotment of rents from a barn, meadows and pastures which he purchased in the Piccadilly area of Manchester. Trustees wisely administered this land on short term leases (4) and made new investments so that the annual income of the charity had grown to over £9,000 in 1891 and, eighty years later, now exceeds £190,000, from which over 1,500 elderly citizens receive weekly pay.

Suitable housing having become a problem for many older people, the distributors of the charity are currently engaged in providing carefully planned estates as at Humphrey Booth Gardens, Mainprice Close, Shelmerdine Gardens (6) and Winstanley Close, each name having an association with trustees of the charity. Nearly a million pounds has already been devoted to the provision of almost 400 homes and others are now being built. The aesthetic quality of their design is indicated by Civic Trust awards.

Midwood Hall, part of the Mainprice Close estate (3), is becoming a focal point for many activities associated with the welfare of the group of Salfordians who were Humphrey's concern.

2

ANNO DECIMO SEXTO

Georgii III. Regis.

C A P. LV.

An Act to enable the Truftees of certain Charity Lands, belonging to the Poor of *Salford*,
in the County Palatine of *Lancafter*, to grant
Building-leafes thereof.

WHEREAS, by Indenture of Grant or
Feoffment, bearing Date the Eighteenth
Day of February, in the Sixth Year of
the Reign of his late Majefty King
Charles the Firft, Humphrey Booth the
elder of Salford in the County of Lan-
cafter Gentleman, did grant, enfeoff, and confirm, unto
Adam Byrom, Thomas Mort, Adam Pilkington, John
Lownds, George Crannage the younger, and John Whit-
worth, therein named and defcribed, their Heirs and
Affigns, for ever, all that Barn, with the Appurtenances,
fituate, ftanding, and being, in Manchefter, in the faid
County of Lancafter, in or near unto the Highway or
Lane leading between the Town of Manchefter aforefaid
and a certain Place near thereunto adjoining, commo-**4**ly

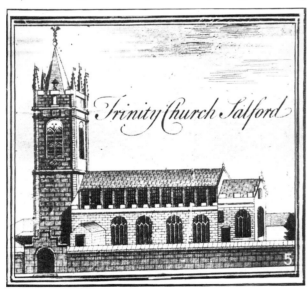

FARMING

It was not until the nineteen thirties that farming ceased within the Salford boundaries. Towards the end, pastures were used for fattening store cattle and the Hodges were so engaged from Kersal Hall (1), the farm buildings being demolished in 1936. In the same year, cows still passed along Broom Lane (4), off Bury New Road.

Farming had been an important nineteenth-century occupation with dairy farms in most of the western districts, as could be seen at Weaste in 1870 (2). The Clowes estates in Broughton and Kersal derived income from farm leases (5) and produce from the home farm (8).

At Pendleton, on the site of Irwell Valley School, the old dairy and farm buildings of New Hall stood until 1926 (3). The barn of Claremont Farm, which preceded Claremont Open Air School, was fired in a Civil Defence exercise in 1939 while Sommerville Farm and barn, shown at the bottom of Bank Lane in 1950 (6), was cleared for house building in 1971. There are various legendary stories about the great barn at Ordsall (7) but it certainly had a threshing floor in earlier days.

No reference to Salford farming would be complete without mention of T. B. Bayley of Hope Hall, who carried out and reported on many important farming experiments (9) and was a founder of what became the Royal Lancashire Agricultural Society. Street names throughout the town, such as Meadow Road, Blackfield Lane, Knoll Street and Barn Street (10), stem from vanished farms and fields. Bandy Lands Lane, by the present Camp Street, was lost when houses were built and Great Cheetham Street became the new name for Cow Lane but Oldfield Road still recalls the 'ouldfeeld' of 1602, which had some form of strip cultivation.

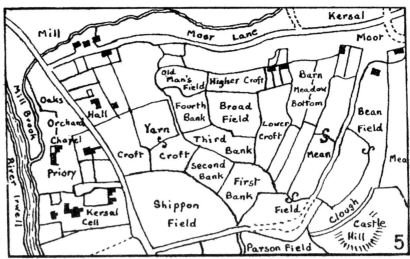

THOUGHTS
on the
Necessity and Advantages of Care and Œconomy
in
COLLECTING AND PRESERVING
different
SUBSTANCES FOR MANURE.

Addressed to the MEMBERS of the
AGRICULTURE SOCIETY
of
Manchester,

October the 12th, 1795.

HAMLETS

The area outside the small town developed in typical country fashion with focal points in scattered villages and hamlets. Larger clusters of houses were on the main highways out of Manchester, at Pendleton and Irlam's-o'th-Height (5) on the Bolton road and at Cheetham Hill on the Bury road where the old settlement was called Tetlow Fold (7, 8). The main roads through the last two became shopping centres which are still

known as 'the village' by older inhabitants although clearance orders are now destroying this character.

A map of 1787 (1) shows the hamlets in the north of Salford. 'Fold' was the Lancashire term for small groups of cottages which might even be too small to qualify as hamlets and Land o'Nod (2), a Weaste fold near present-day Derby Road, also had a typical Lancastrian name. The neighbouring fold of Wardleworth, by Hope Church, was still standing in the nineteen thirties (6). In the fifties, twenty years before their clearance for the massive Ellor Street re-development, roofing work on single storey shops facing Pendleton Town Hall had revealed the existence of the original thatched roofs of village cottages beneath the later slate covering (3).

At Broughton, demolition has encroached on Ford Street cottages (4) which formed part of the hamlet which grew up by the river crossing on the road from Pendleton to Broughton. Here was the centre of activities for Broughton, the manor court meeting at the Griffin Inn near the constables' 'lock up' which was in Ford Street. The book of proceedings of the court, beginning in 1703, gives some idea of day-to-day life in one of these rural hamlets.

ROADS

Country lanes, often still called 'lanes' but no longer rural, linked the hamlets and isolated farmhouses (e.g. Springfield Lane, Bank Lane, Broom Lane, Tanners Lane, Tetlow Lane, Broughton Lane, Hodge Lane). Views such as that of Moor Lane in 1905 (1), show that some were still country lanes in this century and Blackfield Lane, though partly walled in 1840, is only losing this character in 1972 (3).

Main roads to the south were approached through Manchester and the chief road through Salford was the forerunner of the present A6 which was turnpiked in 1752 (4, 6), with a tollbar at the Woolpack (5). The important road to Liverpool branched off here (8) and, though now known as Eccles Old Road, was formerly Sandy Lane. This busy junction has recently resulted in Salford's most ambitious road scheme to date (10). The other road from Manchester to the north was the old Bury road, passing through the northernmost tip of Salford, and a second route was opened when Bury New Road was created as a turnpike, in 1831, with a toll gate at Kersal Bar (9).

As is usual, roads have been of prime importance in governing building development. Growth of the town was first by ribbon building outward along the main roads. Houses then spread along the cross roads, as on Cross Lane in 1820 (7), and this was followed by infilling with new streets and dwellings as estates were built, with scores of miles of 'setted' roads in the nineteenth century (2).

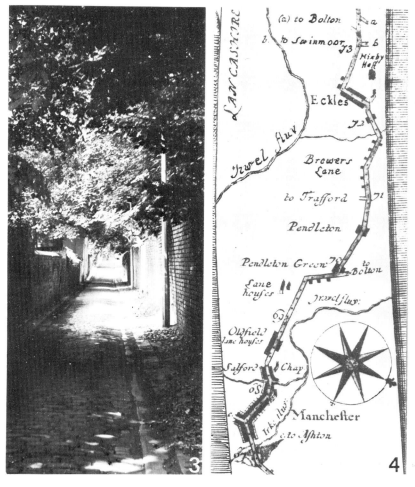

24

TURNPIKES.——Notice is hereby given, that the General Adjourned Meeting of the Trustees of Pendleton, Agecroft, Irlam's o'th' Height, Swinton, Irlam and Gilda Brook Turnpikes, will be held at the Bull's Head Inn, in Manchester, on Thursday the ninth day of July next; at eleven o'clock in the forenoon : when and where the TOLLS arising and to be collected at the several Turnpike Gates, erected near the Wool Pack, in Pendlebury, called Irlam's o'th' Height Turnpike, and near Agecroft Bridge, called Agecroft Turnpike, *Will be LET by AUCTION*, for one year, from the following days, to wit, Irlam's o'th' Height Turnpike from the 13th. day of August next, and Agecroft Turnpike from the 17th. day of the same month, to the highest bidders, in manner directed by the Act passed in the 13th. year of the reign of his present Majesty, "For regulating the turnpike roads :" which tolls arising and to be collected at Irlam's o'th' Height Turnpike, were let the last year at the rent of £722; and which tolls arising and to be collected at Agecroft Turnpike, at the rent of £95, over and above the expences of collecting the same, and will be put up at those respective sums.

Whoever happens to be the best bidder must at the same time give security, with sufficient sureties, to the satisfaction of the trustees then present, for payment of the rent agreed for, and at such times as they shall direct : and it is to be observed, that the biddings of no person will be received unless he shall be prepared with such good and sufficient sureties.

The taker of the tolls arising from Agecroft Turnpike will be allowed to erect side bars, on the road between Singleton Brook and Kersal Moor, and to take tolls thereat from the Sunday next before Whitsunday till the Sunday next but one after.

JAMES COOKE,
Clerk to the said Trustees.

Salford, 12th. June, 1812.

6

5

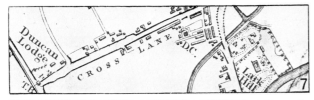

7

9

10

25

DOMESTIC INDUSTRY

The portmote records mention many domestic craftsmen and the home worker persisted in some trades long after the factory system was established. Skill was passed on through the apprenticeship system (3) and Lark Hill Place, in Salford Museum, preserves relics of a craft which was never fully mechanised but has almost died out (1).

There was an early textile industry in south Lancashire based on woollens with linen and then cotton mixtures. During the second half of the eighteenth century, cotton yarns and fabrics assumed prime importance and spinning and weaving were done at home. Until recently, the wide windows of upper floor weaving shops, such as those formerly on Greengate (6), were to be seen around Chapel Street.

The domestic phase of the related bleaching and dyeing trades was undertaken in small workshops attached to dwellings. Cloth was spread out in fields (bleach crofts) as part of the bleaching process and Pendleton was a main centre (9). Dye houses were usually near the river into which waste liquor was run (5), and the Salford side of the Irwell, near Greengate, was lined with semi-domestic workshops in the early nineteenth century (7).

Innkeepers were another group who often manufactured their own products and traces of the King's Arms brewhouse, on Oldfield Road, can be seen behind the tavern (4).

By 1788, when most domestic industries were about to give way to the factory system, Salford had grown little since 1650 but the beginning of the industrial spread towards the river and along the Liverpool road could be seen (2).

A street name (8) is a reminder of the whitsters or bleachers who occupied river sites towards Agecroft while nearby Laundry Street (and the now demolished Washerwoman's Arms!) commemorated the numerous later washerwomen of Brindle Heath who served the well-to-do residents of Pendleton.

WHIT LANE·6 8

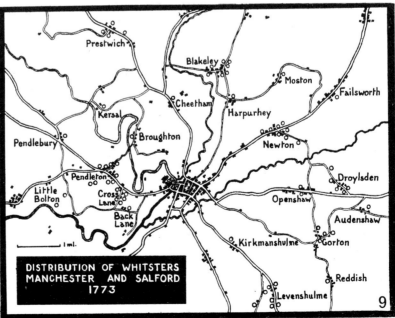

DISTRIBUTION OF WHITSTERS MANCHESTER AND SALFORD 1773 9

WATER POWER

Factories superseded domestic work-shops when power was used to drive machines and new machinery was invented to take advantage of a power drive. The earliest widespread source of power was falling water and mills were built by natural falls or artificially created heads of water, which had the additional advantage of impounding a reserve of water.

Water mills for corn milling were commonest and Mode Wheel Mill (1) on the Irwell and Kersal Mill, below a millpond on Singleton Brook (2), had a long life. The first big cotton spinning factories utilised this source of power which, in Salford, meant the use of weirs on the river. Ackers' mill at the Crescent and the notorious William Douglas's mill at Pendleton (3, 4) were the first. Douglas Green and Mode Wheel Road today recall these former water-powered mills. Original weirs may still be seen at Pendleton and the Crescent but the Mode Wheel weir has been replaced by Ship Canal locks which raise vessels to the Salford terminal docks.

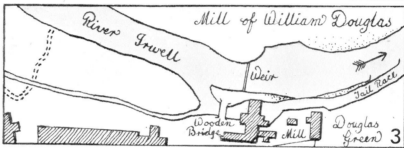

COAL

Rapid factory development followed the perfection of the steam engine and sources of coal were an important factor in their location. The thick coal seams of west Salford and the Irwell valley provided excellent supplies and from Pendleton Pit (1) it was a short haul, by road or canal, to new works in Salford. Many mills were sited beside the Bolton and Bury Canal, at Pendleton (2), where coal could be unloaded direct to boiler-houses. At the Salford terminus of the canal extensive coal yards were established and, by 1830, textile mills had been erected close by (3, A: Walker's silk mill and cotton mills of B: Islington Twist Co., C: Gough, D: Slater, E: Smith & Rawson, F: Brotherton, G: Higgins).

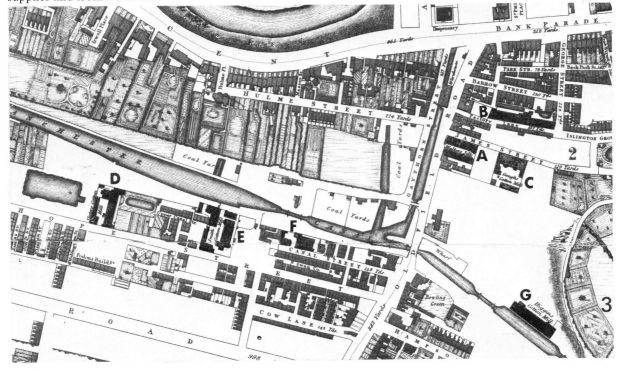

WATERWAYS

The growth of the factory system was bound up with improved communications and poor roads were largely replaced for goods transport, in the industrial areas, by newly created waterways. The Irwell and Mersey were made navigable after 1720 and an early quay was at Salford (1) while later river improvements, after canals became competitors, greatly increased river traffic downstream of New Bailey Bridge (2). Passenger services to Runcorn and Liverpool sailed from the adjacent landing stage, seen in 1908 (3).

Canals, planned to serve coalfields and ports, expedited industrial development and the prototype Bridgewater Canal, by its first Act of 1759, intended to terminate in Salford (5), as recalled by street names (6). The Manchester, Bolton and Bury Canal did lock down to the river near Ordsall Lane (4) and, from 1794, narrow coal boats and wide cargo barges (7) served Salford. A hundred years later the modern Ship Canal dug terminal docks in Ordsall so that ocean-going vessels now tie up alongside Trafford Road (8) and Salford has become a major port.

TRICESIMO SECUNDO

GEORGII II. REGIS.

....

Cap. 2.

An Act to enable the Most Noble *Francis* Duke of *Bridgewater* to make a navigable Cut or Canal from a certain Place in the Township of *Salford* to or near *Worsley Mill* and *Middlewood* in the Manor of *Worsley*, and to or near a Place called *Hollin Ferry*, in the County Palatine of *Lancaster*.

WHEREAS by an Act made in the Tenth Year of the Reign of His present Majesty, intituled *An Act for making navigable the River or Brook called* Worsley Brook, *from* Worsley Mill, *in the Township of* Worsley *in the County Palatine of* Lancaster, *to the River* Irwell *in the said County*, (reciting that the making and keeping the said River or Brook navigable and passable for Boats and other Vessels would be very beneficial to Trade, advantageous to the Poor, and convenient for the Carriage of Coal, Stone, Timber, and other Goods, Wares, and Merchandizes, to and from the said Places and Parts adjacent, and answer many other good Purposes,) certain Persons therein named were appointed and empowered to undertake and complete the said Navigation ; but the Persons so appointed have hitherto neglected to carry the said Act into Execution, whereby the Public hath been deprived of the Benefit A thereby

10 G. 2. c. 9.

5

4

7

WORSLEY ST. 3

6

MANCHESTER DOCKS

8

TEXTILE INDUSTRY

Before cotton superseded woollens and linens, Salford was a textile manufacturing and trading centre with a cloth hall in Greengate, replaced by a new one at the foot of Victoria Bridge (1), in 1814.

With the advent of cotton and mechanisation, expansion of the industry, and the textile towns, was accelerated. Small workshops were replaced by steam-driven mills, such as Langworthy Bros. (2), and bleachers and dyers such as Barge's of the Aldelphi (5) competed for riverside sites to facilitate waste disposal. Canalside location was good for water and coal and Brotherton's Mill near Oldfield Road (3) and Elkanah Armitage's mills from 1840 at Pendleton (6) illustrate this phase of development.

When railways came, cotton mills were built near them, that of Ermen & Engels by the Liverpool and

32

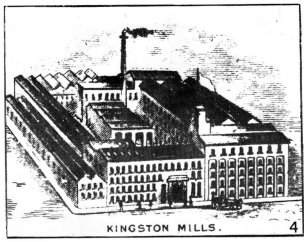

KINGSTON MILLS.

Manchester line, at Weaste, while Wright Turner & Son, established in 1833, erected the Kingston Mill (4) by the Bolton Railway.

Urbanisation of Ordsall came in the later nineteenth century when the river was lined with factories, Haworth's spinning mill (7) and weaving sheds having over 4,000 workpeople. After re-equipment in 1960–63, auction of the machinery in 1972 attracted many scrap metal merchants (8).

FOUNDRIES

Rapid growth of the cotton industry had repercussions on many other industries and services. The new machines often had wooden framing and working parts but advantages of metal were quickly realised, small foundries were established in most of the textile towns and the ten brass and ironfounders in Salford, by 1850, were joined by others in Pendleton (3) in the second half of the century. Cast iron had been used architecturally and Salford foundries produced bollards (1), lamp-posts and railings (2) but, again, the cotton industry fostered developments as the pioneer iron-framed spinning mill of Phillips & Lee, on Chapel Street, inaugurated a demand for pillars and beams to combat the fire risks of timber supports and joists. Simultaneously, the use of steam engines on Watt's principle kept foundries busy, with Bateman & Sherratt, ironfounders before 1800, pirating patents and taking a leading role. Later specialist engineers usually made their own castings, Hodgkinson's, by Pendleton Church (4), having a separate foundry near Liverpool Street. Excellent moulding sand was quarried in Salford in 1937 (5), along Eccles New Road.

34

ENGINEERING

The metal trades were expanded to meet the millowners' needs and many ironfounders became millwrights, who were known as engineers as their scope widened still further. William Higgins, with an extensive millwright's shop off Gravel Lane (5), was also a cotton mill owner and the world-renowned firm of Mather & Platt grew from a Salford foundry (2). George Wilson & Co., with two works in Springfield Lane (1), were typical of many other engineers whose shorter life coincided with the boom period in the cotton industry. Some have vanished without trace, others have left only a name in Salford (4, 6, 7, 8), some continue as part of larger concerns (3) and a few, like Sir James Farmer Norton Ltd., founded in 1852, still carry on with an unchanged name in modernized works on their original site (9).

CHEMICALS

A.D. 1854 . . . . . . Nº 153.

Manufacture of the Prussiates of Potash and Soda.

LETTERS PATENT to Peter Spence, of Pendleton, near Manchester, in the County of Lancaster, Manufacturing Chemist, for the Invention of " IMPROVEMENTS IN MANUFACTURING THE PRUSSIATES OF POTASH AND SODA."

Sealed the 18th July 1854, and dated the 21st January 1854.

PROVISIONAL SPECIFICATION left by the said Peter Spence at the Office of the Commissioners of Patents, with his Petition, on the 21st January 1854.

I, PETER SPENCE, do hereby declare the nature of the said Invention for " IMPROVEMENTS IN MANUFACTURING THE PRUSSIATES OF POTASH AND SODA " to be as follows :—

The object of this Invention is to effect the manufacture of prussiates of potash and soda in a more economic manner than heretofore. To this end I

The early chemical industry was also closely linked with textiles. Chemical bleaching encouraged numerous chemical works, one of the best known at the beginning of the nineteenth century being Varley's, on Whit Lane, which was combined with a bleachworks. Nearby, in mid-century, was the Pendleton Alum Works of Spence & Dixon, the former probably being Salford's most famous chemist (2). Before synthetics, vegetable dyes from Ordsall (4) supplied calico printers while starch and soap makers catered for the finishing trades. Hervey's, Goodwin's and Thom's were forerunners of the toilet soap firms of Cussons (5) and Colgate–Palmolive. For about 25 years, from 1915, Boot's occupied a large pharmaceutical works on Adelphi Street (1) and were succeeded by the Pendleton makers of Kruschen Salts before closure after take-over by Aspro. Later chemical firms using coal tar and petroleum raw materials were established by the Ship Canal (3).

BREWING

A tax and a malt monopoly by the Irk mills in Manchester resulted in the setting up of breweries in the surrounding townships. Following the early phase of brewhouses attached to the inns, many small firms were established in Salford, several favouring a site near the Irwell (1). There was a gradual rationalization and reduction in number so that, by 1900, with good water from deep borings in the underlying sandstone, six firms were brewing with Groves & Whitnall, Walker & Homfrays and Threlfalls being known over a wide area, the latter's beer being well publicised in Eccles (2). Bottles dug up in Swinton (3) recall the related soft drinks firm of Townsends (5) with works in Paradise, Greengate. Modern take-overs resulted in more closures and, when the parent firm switched the Groves & Whitnall production to Warrington, in 1972, a single brewery was left (4) and this long-established industry may soon be unrepresented in the town. The defunct Mottram's Brewery left two street names behind (6).

HOMES FOR WORKERS

Poorer townsmen have always tended towards multiple occupation of older houses which had been built for wealthier tenants, as happened first in Greengate (1). Early nineteenth-century workers sought homes near their employment and the boatmen's houses near the terminus of the Bolton & Bury Canal (3) were at least airy. More typically, near the industrial quarters of the town, maximum numbers of cheap and poorly-built houses were crowded on minimum space and behind the main streets in the Greengate, Town Hall and Liverpool Street districts were hundreds of back-to-back houses (4). Access was from narrow streets (5) and courts (5, 6), water supply was communal (W. T. in 5) and closets were shared even in the less closely-

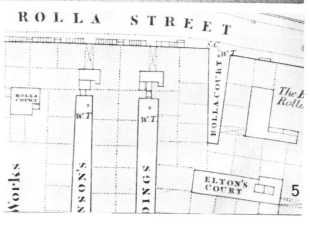

packed terraced houses fronting the streets near Salford Cathedral (8). Cellar dwellings were also common in working-class areas of Salford and Pendleton (7).

The pawnbroker played a significant part in these communities but Salford Township's 52 pawnbrokers of a century ago had dwindled to three in 1972. One had lost the well-known symbol, another was two-thirds attenuated (2) and the third continued under the same sign and name (9) and with the same Greengate location that it had in 1862 when there were six pawnbrokers' shops in this street.

HOMES FOR MANCUNIANS

The first factories of the steam age were in central Manchester and Salford, near the homes of the workers, and the commercial centre grew up round the Exchange. Factory owners and merchants also lived in the town but moved out as smoke pollution became offensive. Salford, Pendleton and Broughton, in the lee of the prevailing winds, were favoured residential districts and this westward drift has continued to the present time. From the end of the eighteenth century, some residents in Georgian houses on the Crescent (1) worked in Manchester. Eccles Old Road, with houses set in spacious estates overlooking the Cheshire Plain, attracted wealthier merchants, Buile Hill (2) being built for Sir Thomas Potter, first mayor of Manchester. The Heywoods, important Manchester bankers, had several homes near this road each with its coach house and stables (4) to provide transport into the town before the motor car era. As portrayed in 'Hobson's Choice', it

seems that the Mancunians on this road would make purchases at the craftsmen's shops on Chapel Street, Salford (3).

Nineteenth-century merchants from many parts of the world were attracted to 'Cottonopolis' and tended to live in groups which established their own cultural activities. The eastern Mediterranean community had settled around Bury New Road, at Higher Broughton (5), by 1850, and the Greek Church (6) is a reminder of this colony.

Judges from Manchester Assize and Crown Courts have lodged at Kersal (7) and, nearby, the modern 'Bishopscourt' (8) has recently replaced a Victorian house as the home of the Bishop of Manchester. Even today, notable newcomers to Manchester find it convenient to reside in Salford. The new manager for Manchester United finds a house on Eccles Old Road (9) midway between Old Trafford and the practice ground in Broughton where strategy for success is evolved.

41

RAILWAYS

As in the Irwell Street area (4), railways covered a large proportion of Salford and extensive sidings such as those at New Bailey Street Goods Yard in 1936 (3) influenced its town plan. It was appropriate that the last scheduled steam train in Britain passed through the town in 1968 (2) on the same Liverpool and Manchester line which was traversed by the first regular steam-hauled passenger train in 1830 (1). The original Act for this railway planned a terminus in Salford and a few stone sleepers in Ordsall Lane (5) are reminders of George Stephenson's work. The Manchester, Bolton and Bury line, opened in 1838, did have its first terminus in Salford (7) until it was carried to Victoria Station, in Manchester, by extensions of the existing viaducts (4) over potentially valuable parts of Salford and with ill effects on future planning.

With the abandonment of railway lines, goods yards, engine and carriage sheds, stations and other associated works, sites are now available for other purposes and planners can seize the opportunities for modern re-development.

New Bailey Street Yard provides a useful car park (6), until a massive building scheme commences, and Irwell Street Yard is ripe for development (7). Most significant, in 1972, is the proposed abandonment of two of the four tracks of the Liverpool and Manchester line to provide a route through Salford for the South Lancashire motorway.

TRAVELLING

BY THE

MANCHESTER, BOLTON & BURY

RAILWAY,

1838.

The following, until further notice, will be the times of Departure:

FROM MANCHESTER TO BOLTON.

Station, New Bailey-Street, Salford.

First Train	....Seven A.M.
Second do.	....Half-past Eight A.M.
Third do.	....Half-past Nine A.M.
Fourth do.	....Twelve Noon.
Fifth do.	....Three P.M.
Sixth do.	....Five P.M.
Seventh do.	....Seven P.M.

ON SUNDAYS.

| First Train | ....Eight A.M. |
| Second do. | ....Six P.M. |

FARES.

First Class Coach, 2s. 6d.; Second Class Coach, 2s. Children under Seven years of Age Half Price.

FROM BOLTON TO MANCHESTER.

Station, Bridgeman-Street, Bolton.

First Train	....Seven A.M.
Second do.	....Half-past Eight A.M.
Third do.	....Half-past Nine A.M.
Fourth do.	....Twelve Noon.
Fifth do.	....Three P.M.
Sixth do.	....Five P.M.
Seventh do.	....Seven P.M.

ON SUNDAYS.

| First Train | ....Nine A.M. |
| Second do. | ....Seven P.M. |

FARES.

First Class Coach 2s. 6d.; Second Class Coach 2s. Children under Seven Years of Age Half Price.

REGULATIONS.

The Doors of the Booking Office will be closed precisely at the time appointed for starting, after which no Passenger can be admitted.

BOOKING.

There will be no Booking Place, except at the Company's Offices at the respective Stations in Manchester and Bolton.

LUGGAGE.

Each Passenger's Luggage will be placed on the Roof of the Coach in which he has taken his place; Carpet Bags and small Luggage may be placed under the seat.

No charge for Luggage belonging to the Passenger under 70lbs. weight; above that a charge will be made of one halfpenny per pound for the whole distance.

The attention of Travellers is requested to the Legal Notice exhibited at the Stations respecting the limitation of the Company's Liabilities to the Loss or Damage of Luggage.

CONDUCTORS, GUARDS, & PORTERS.

Every Train is provided with a Guard and a Conductor, who is responsible for the order and regularity of the journey.

The Company's Porters will load and unload the Luggage, and put it into or upon any Omnibus or other carriage at the stations. No Fees or Gratuities allowed to conductors, Guards, Porters, or other Persons in the service of the company.

No smoking allowed in the carriages or stations.

No person will be allowed to sell Liquors or Eatables of any kind upon the Line.

PARCELS.

The charge for Parcels will be regulated by weight and size.

TRAVELLING TO THE NORTH.

Passengers may be booked at the company's station, in Manchester, for all parts of the North.

*Railway Office, Bolton-Street, Salford,
29th May 1838.*

7

5

6

8

TRAMWAYS

While railway works influenced the layout of the town, the two lines into Manchester were also responsible for some out-of-town housing for people who commuted from stations such as Weaste, Seedley, Pendleton, Irlam's-o'th-Height and, in the early days, even Cross Lane. But a much more important factor in determining suburban development was the pattern of public road transport which grew up from about 1825.

John Greenwood, of the Woolpack Inn, inaugurated services with a box-like bus running between Pendleton and Market St., Manchester (1). A three-horse bus, carrying four times as many passengers, was introduced by a competitor in 1852 and Greenwood's company was forced to follow suit. In 1865, the latter amalgamated with the rival company to form the Manchester Carriage Co., and one of its larger vehicles is depicted passing the Pendleton office of this concern (2). Although fares were reduced by 50 per cent, they were still beyond the purse of workmen and resultant building near the bus routes was of 'villa' residences for merchants and professional men.

In 1877, a tramway was laid from Pendleton to Manchester and along Bury New Road to the Grove Inn, on the Broughton boundary, and later extended to Kersal (3). The system quickly spread and better services aided the growth of Pendleton (10) and Lower Broughton suburbs. Bus and tram interests united in 1880 as the Manchester Carriage & Tramways Co. with depots and stables catering for Salford at Pendleton, Weaste, Lower Broughton and Market Place, Higher Broughton (8). The Corporation took over the tramways in 1901 and electrification soon followed, with central organisation at Frederick Road depot (4). Speedy journeys at two miles for a penny (9) pushed suburban housing to the borough boundary at the Height and Higher Broughton.

A cross-city route was introduced

with a motor bus service from Great Cheetham Street, Broughton, to Pendleton in 1920 (5) and the ease with which new bus routes could be introduced helped estate develop-

ments at Littleton Road, Lancaster Road, and, later, Sommerville Road. Suburban patterns of housing and of new roads like Leicester Road, were largely fashioned by the tramways

and these, in turn, pre-determined bus routes when buses replaced trams. Former transport chiefs, from the days of the Carriage Co., are still remembered at Pendleton (6, 7).

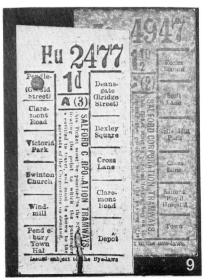

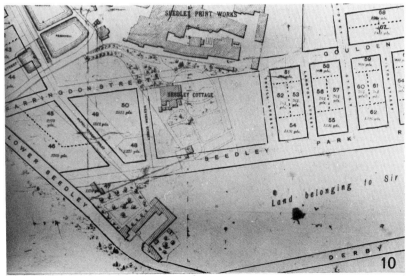

The elected officials of the Portmote Court controlled the affairs of the town under the terms of the original charter and shared with the Salford Hundred Court (1) the court house in the market place (2). Self-appointed joint Commissioners for Manchester and Salford replaced the Portmote in 1795 but soon divided into two bodies, the Salford group leaving the court house, about 1809, for rented Town's Offices in Chapel Street. The privately financed Town Hall was completed in 1827 (5) and an Act of 1829 constituted separate Commissioners for Salford. They purchased the Town Hall in 1834 and it was first enlarged after the town was incorporated in 1844. Elections for the borough, and the parliamentary constituency established in 1832, produced many hard hitting posters (6).

With civic pride, in 1873, a new main thoroughfare was to be called Corporation Road, but took the name of a leading Alderman (3) and this practice has recently been revived (4).

PARKS

As urban development spread outward, first signs of a concern for the environment were shown by several public-spirited men. Wealthier citizens could relax in the Zoological Gardens on Bury New Road and less fortunate townsmen might sample country pleasures when attending races, military reviews or hangings on Kersal Moor. It was a happy coincidence that the last races there, at Whitsuntide 1846, were followed in August by the opening of Lark Hill, later Peel Park (1), the first of three public parks established by subscription in Manchester and Salford. These were very formal and, apart from a gymnasium and archery butts, were designed for a *Keep off the Grass* philosophy. As football became popular, scarcity of grassland was met by cinder pitches on recreation grounds as at Hadfield Street Rec, Teneriffe Street Rec (2), Spike Island and Liverpool Street Rec, which were unfenced rectangular areas among the rows of terraced houses. Later parkland, at Buile Hill and Clowes Park (3) has skilfully preserved natural features and enhanced them by further landscaping.

47

EXPANSION

Parliamentary reform, in 1832, gave Salford its first M.P. and formed a parliamentary division (1) by joining the growing urban area with the still rural Broughton (2) and with the village nucleus and ribbon accretion of suburban residences for townsmen at Pendleton (3). Local government was still separately administered.

As houses and factories spread,

COUNTY BOROUGH OF SALFORD.

REPORT

OF THE

COMMITTEE APPOINTED BY THE COUNCIL

TO CONSIDER THE

REPORT OF THE ASSOCIATION,

FOR THE CONSIDERATION OF THE

AMALGAMATION

OF

MANCHESTER AND SALFORD.

boundaries between the three townships were more clearly marked (8) and local officials regularly beat the bounds. These township boundaries exerted odd influences on building lay-out up to the present period of large-scale re-development (7). In 1853, after several abortive attempts, the townships were amalgamated. A loosely federated system of local government was administered from town halls in Bexley Square, Duke Street (4) and the new Pendleton building shown in the architect's drawing of 1867 (6). By this time, the spread of buildings towards the north, west and south was quite marked (9).

On several occasions, the feasibility of linking Salford and Manchester was considered but there was never any real sign that this would be successful and Salford opinion has consistently been against such a move (5).

6

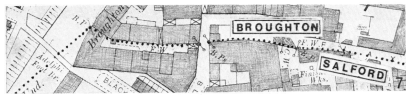

7

8

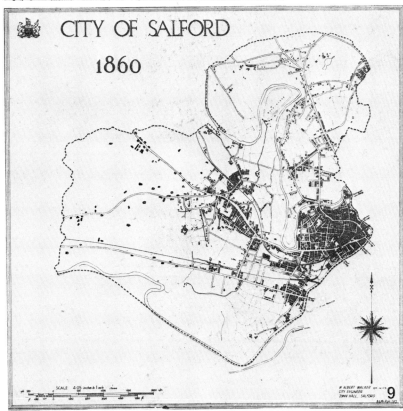

CITY OF SALFORD

1860

9

49

BYE-LAW HOUSING

With enforced demolition of some of the worst slums, the first efforts to secure improved standards of housing were made through the passing of bye-laws. Houses were still built, for renting (7), by private firms and the majority adopted minimum legal requirements. Compulsory ventilation at the back of houses created miles of 'tunnel back' dwellings off Eccles New Road (1) and elsewhere (3), but the frontages gradually improved in appearance, as at Blandford Street (2), with wider roads required by later bye-laws. Private builders often adopted grouped names for neighbouring streets, such as Ash, Laburnum, Alder, Fir, etc., and the builder who used the family names of Jane, Frances and George Henry was determined to include himself (4). Another builder, off Cross Lane, decided to be equally brief (5). Owners of estates which were ripe for development financed means of linking them to the town. Clowes' Broughton Bridge, of 1806, and Fitzgerald's suspension Bridge (6), of 1826, at first resulted in expensive houses and then extensive bye-law property.

6

As at Cleminson Street, in 1930 (9), the corner shop was a universal feature of terraced housing development. It had a social function, often including a credit system which would operate, near Broughton Bridge (8), after the great flood of 1866. The Council began to show concern about the indiscriminate mixture of housing and industry (3) and, in 1914, adopted a town planning scheme (10) for 2,000 acres which were still available for building purposes.

8

9

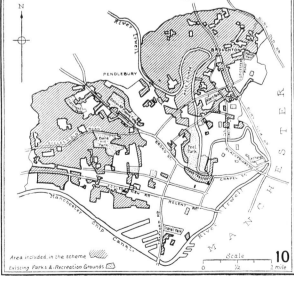

10

VARIED INDUSTRY

Though main growth was due to cotton and its allied trades, Salford has been fortunate that there was early diversification of industry. It was logical that textiles should be made up in the area and numerous varied clothing manufacturing firms were set up, particularly in Broughton (2). An early rubber industry developed (3) and, again, waterproofing of cloth and rainwear manufacture were a natural outcome. Rubber-covered cables were also produced from 1880 (1) to meet demands of the new age of electricity. A number of firms which started in a small way (4) later achieved international importance.

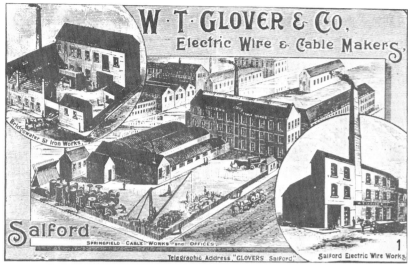

Many electrical engineering firms also commenced operations at this time and other engineers began to specialise (8). The motor age, with a first Salford registration in 1904 (5), saw the short-lived Horbick car made in Pendleton.

Several paper firms, such as Carver-Walker (6), were important in special fields and newer types of chemical concerns, like Berry Wiggins (7), came with the Ship Canal. Salfordians have always been employed in diverse aspects of the entertainment industry catering for a wide area (10) and Brewery, Foundry, Cable, Dyer and other Streets (9) take their names from former nearby crafts.

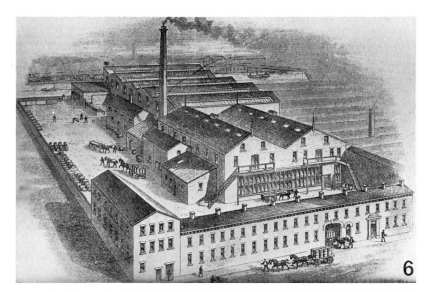

BETWEEN THE WARS

THE SUTTON DWELLINGS SALFORD

THESE DWELLINGS WERE ERECTED
UNDER THE CHARITABLE TRUSTS
OF THE WILL OF
WILLIAM RICHARD SUTTON
OF GOLDEN LANE LONDON E C
CARRIER
WHO DIED 20TH MAY 1900

After being granted County Borough status in 1888, Salford became a City in 1926 and the building of houses began on the few larger remaining undeveloped areas. Council house estates at Tootal Drive and Lower Kersal (1) were mainly in blocks of two or four houses with ill-planned open spaces at the rear. The Sutton Trust demolished large old properties at Pendleton to build the first extensive estate of flats (2) while the Showmen's Guild maintained a tradition of wintering on various open spaces (6). Private semi-detached houses, with typical lay-out (3), were erected on the western borders of the town with communities of owner-occupiers (5), and the first signs of modernism appeared in the designs of a few detached houses in Broughton Park (4,7). Mobile shopping (8) was introduced to most of these newer estates. In 1939, Sir John Anderson was responsible for a further new type of temporary accommodation which appeared in many gardens, as behind Tootal Road (9).

55

CHANGING INDUSTRY

In most areas where the industrial revolution originated the staple industries are in decline as new materials and techniques are introduced and competition increases.

In Salford, coal mining finished in 1939 and, by 1971, cotton had practically vanished as successive closures followed that of Broughton Flax Mill (1). Ample floor space in an urban area meant that abandoned mills were potential warehouses and such a conversion is to be seen next to the flax mill (5). Some disused mills were demolished for site value but others were divided among a number of smaller firms. Thus, signs outside the former Salford Electrical Instruments works, on Silk Street, indicate that it now has at least ten occupants (6).

Wartime bombing destroyed some factories and, while Lord's Tar Works overcame the effects of a delayed action bomb at Weaste (7), firms like W. H. Bailey were forced out of the town. To stop flooding in Lower Broughton a £2¼m. scheme was carried out. Factories which had encroached on the Irwell were removed and the sharp left-hand U-bend at Springfield Lane became a gradual curve to the right with consequent elimination of more works and a change in the vista from Broughton Bridge between 1951 and 1971 (2, 3). Industry and housing were inextricably mixed up in pre-war Salford and zoning in the new town plan has meant the demolition of some factories, such as Turner's near Cross Lane (4). New roads also affect industrial premises, sixteen of which will be cleared for the M602.

Rationalisation associated with take-overs has eliminated many old Salford firms. Trafford Mill became part of Fine Spinners & Doublers who were absorbed by Courtaulds and the mill closed in 1971. The next year, Greenall Whitley closed Groves & Whitnall's brewery, started in 1835, to

4

concentrate at Warrington; parent companies switched production to other plants and shut the modern offices of Churchill machine tools, founded in Salford, and the Berry Wiggins oil refinery; and the Carrington Group closed Mandlebergs, pioneers in the waterproof trade, although the Orchard Street works (8) were immediately acquired for conversion to an industrial estate.

6

7

8

COMMERCE

Throughout the nineteenth and the first half of the twentieth century the commercial hub of the south-east Lancashire region was built up on the Manchester side of the Irwell. Pre-existing factories and railways in the centre of Salford prevented office development, except for odd warehouses such as that of Messrs. Baerlein on Blackfriars Street in 1883 (1).

After 1946, bomb damage, clearance, enhanced land values and parking problems changed the position and large-scale commercial developments have begun. 'Out of town' offices were built, as at the Crescent and Pendleton, but the main growth is at the Salford bridgeheads leading into the traditional Manchester commercial centre. Highland House dominates Victoria Bridge (3), Townbury House adjoins Blackfriars Bridge and Manchester's Albert Bridge House now looks across the Irwell to the Salford office blocks of the West Riverside scheme (2).

Opposite the latter, planning approval was given in 1972 for a £9,000,000 complex of offices and shops on the site of the former New Bailey prison and railway yard.

UNIVERSITY CITY

It was natural that an industrial centre such as Salford should lead in technical education. Sir William Mather set an example with a works' school and eloquent advocacy and the early municipal Royal Technical College of 1896 (1) was Salford's show building for many years. It became one of the post-war colleges of advanced technology and enhanced status was gained by an Act and Charter of 1968. The new university, with strong science and technical faculties, is rapidly developing a campus (3) round the Peel Park buildings which will have a marked influence on the city's future. Appropriately, the first Chancellor has been the Duke of Edinburgh (2) who often comments on this technological age at University Court and Congregation.

RACECOURSE

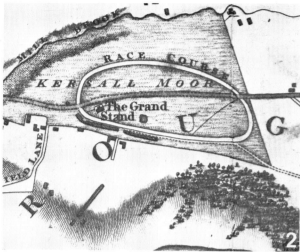

'Manchester Races' were run on Salford courses (2) from inception in the seventeenth century to termination in 1963. The original course (1) moved from Kersal Moor in 1846, switched to New Barns and, when this became Ship Canal docks, in 1902, the races returned to Castle Irwell (4) near the first home. In turn, this became ripe for development and was finally acquired for university purposes. Erection of the first 800 staff and student flats (3) commenced in 1972 but much will remain as an open space.

REORGANISATION

After many discussions on the Maud Report, local government re-organisation produced a unit in the Manchester Metropolitan region which, in mid-1972, was still designated District 12(d) (5).

Irwell and Swinford were two of the unpopular names proposed for the new authority, half of whose inhabitants now reside in Salford, and the rest in Eccles, Swinton and Pendlebury, Worsley and Irlam.

Boundaries had already become indistinct in the mid-twentieth century and had to be signposted (3). Gilda Brook, separating Salford and Eccles and depicted at Victoria Road in 1938 (1), had been built over and Salford gas and transport services, such as the 18 bus route from Manchester towards Worsley (4), had always ignored boundaries to the west although for long they had terminated near the Manchester boundary. Large areas of Worsley and Irlam (2) have housed Salford overspill and standing conference for District 12(d) has located the new administrative centre on the spacious Swinton Town Hall site.

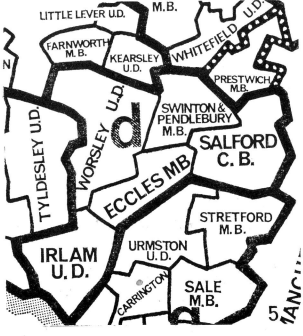

NEW INDUSTRIES

Several old-established firms like P. R. Jackson, now part of the David Brown group and depicted over fifty years ago (1), have modernised their premises and continue to produce old and new products or specialise in one field. Ward & Goldstone have replaced an obsolete cotton mill by a new cable factory (3), have built a computer centre and retain headquarters in Salford. Main roads through the urban area are an obvious location for major car dealers and workshops (4, 5) and vehicle hire (2) and road transport are related growth industries, as also is plastics (7). With over 1000 firms, Salford has many smaller concerns which may occupy adapted workshops, often in converted houses, as in Camp Street (6). Many employ machinists for whom there is a constant demand (10) while new industrial and trading estates at Liverpool Street (8), Eccles New Road, Ordsall (9) and Brindle Heath cater for light industry and warehousing. Logically, Manchester Liners have removed head office from Central Manchester to a site overlooking its vessels in Salford Docks (11).

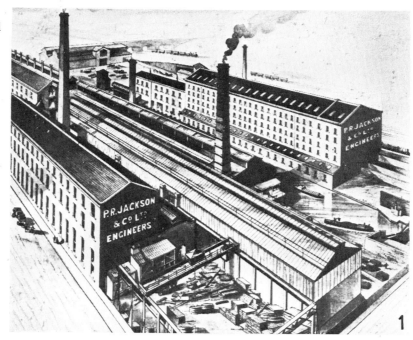

6

THE STYLO PLASTICS &
ENGRAVING CO. LIMITED
REGISTERED OFFICE

7

FACTORIES & WAREHOUSES
TO LET OR FOR SALE
ON THIS ESTATE
and on other estates in MANCHESTER
and throughout the country
apply to the agent on site - or to...
Westminster
construction
COMPANY LIMITED

9

KLEIN BROS
casual wear

THE MANCHESTER WALL & FLOORING

8

10

11

NEW HOUSES

Bomb damage (1) and planned slum clearance (2) have provided large sites for new housing. The first post-war buildings were pre-fabs and other more permanent factory built dwellings on Weaste Lane (3). There were no sites for big private estates and builders were limited to smaller vacant plots, the infilling of gardens around large old houses, as along Singleton Road in 1950 (6), or their demolition and replacement by groups of houses or flats, as seen along Old Hall Road (8). Early Corporation re-development used traditional houses on the Fairhope Estate (4) but, with space at a premium, a period of high rise

building culminated in the Ellor
Street scheme (7), which included
the city shopping precinct (5). By
1972, the changing skyline of the
city can be seen beyond the tower
blocks of the Lower Kersal Estate (9).
By this time, Corporation opinion
was turning away from high rise
flats but private developers were
building flats instead of houses!

NEW VISTAS

The change from a rural to an in-dustrial town has drastically altered almost the whole of the landscape of Salford. Huntsmen can no longer ride over fields around the present Irwell Street as they did 250 years ago (1) and land values have risen enormously with the advent of industry and commerce. The first phase of the multi-million pound development, which stands on the site of the footpath behind the early huntsmen, forms the background to the Irwell Street scene to-day (2). A tower block of 19 storeys will rise on the pools now covering the area over which the fox ran and this office complex will lead to further

appreciation of land values in the central area of Salford with result-ant changes in the character of new buildings.

Even this century has seen remark-able changes in views in the town. It has been the period of revival of the roads, with new ideas in trans-port, and the milkman who could take a short cut along the wrong side of Broad Street by Pendleton Church, in 1901 (3), would find it difficult to do this on the ten lane wide road system now being con-structed at this spot (4)—and equally difficult to recognise anything but the church.

Much thought has been given to modern road schemes so that adverse environmental effects on Salfordians will be minimised. It is to be hoped that similar care will be taken in all changes and even in the design of details. New designs, materials and techniques are in-creasingly introduced for reasons of economy and do not always improve the outlook for the man in the street. Cast iron, as used for fencing at Haworth's Mill on Ordsall Lane (5), is, like the mill itself, a thing of the past but it is questionable whether its modern counterpart (6), round a new factory next door to the demolished mill, has the same visual value.

NEW GENERATIONS

Future development and improvement will be in the context of a New Salford and will lie in the hands of successors of the present generation. To-day's citizens will remember the demolition in the early 1960s of a street (1) adjacent to the Town Hall. In 1840, Number One was occupied by the land agent John Browning and Brunswick Street, behind him, was then fronted by back-to-back dwellings of his generation (2). To-day's rising generation now have a play-ground on their site (3). With his eye for the subtly symbolic picture, Don McPhee, of *The Guardian*, captured in 1972 the earnestness of the young Salfordian who started sweeping away some remaining litter of the past in preparation for the task of her own generation (4).

EYES OF THE ARTIST

Salford pictures by L. S. Lowry (1) and Harold Riley (2), twentieth century artists of international repute, provide a clearer vision of life in Salford than any series of photographs. Part of a 1926 Lowry drawing in the fine Salford Gallery collection of his works (3) records St. George's Church domination of an early twentieth-century children's playground on a typical 'rec' at Charlestown, now built over. A hundred yards from Lowry's viewpoint Riley made his 1961 sketch of now demolished houses, off Whit Lane (4), and perpetuates the atmosphere of a vanished mining-textile community.

SALFORD IN 1794

At the end of the eighteenth century the Salford nucleus still preserved its medieval form and many of its structures. The courthouse and cross stood in the centre of Greengate and half-timbered houses fronted the main streets, some with their original gardens at the rear, but factories had begun to line the river bank and potential slum dwellings were encroaching on the gardens of the older houses near the bridge.

PENDLETON IN 1832

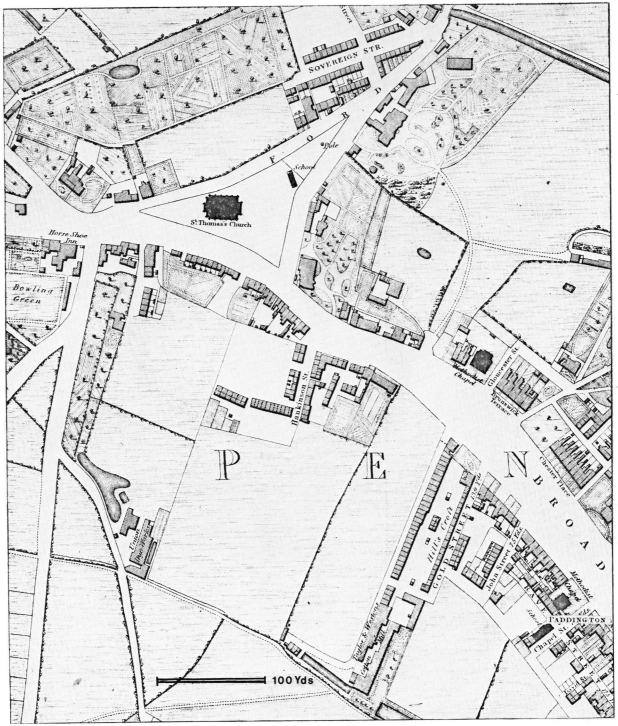

Pendleton clearly showed the village pattern of houses around a green, although the church had moved on to the green from Brindleheath Road in 1831 and the maypole had moved further down Ford Lane. Ribbon building, with Methodist chapels of 1806 and 1810, lined the main road from Salford and the first two mills had resulted in the building of workmen's settlements in the Sovereign Street and Hill's Croft areas.

KERSAL IN 1858

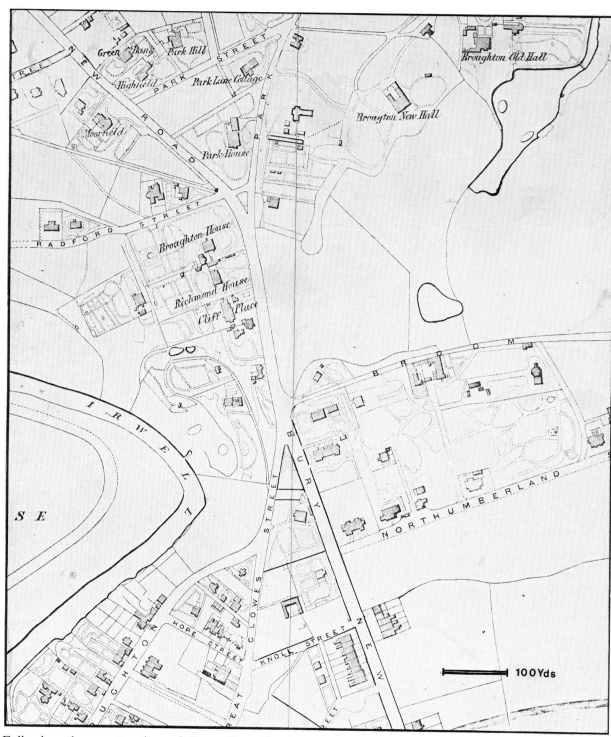

Following the construction of Bury New Road, twenty years earlier, Clowes' lands in Kersal, at the Cliff and around Broughton Hall, were developed with rural 'mansions', those between Northumberland Street and Broom Lane in the former Zoologica Gardens. They were more typically Victorian than th earlier halls on Eccles Old Road and each set in garden which aimed to give a country estate effect.

ORDSALL IN 1872

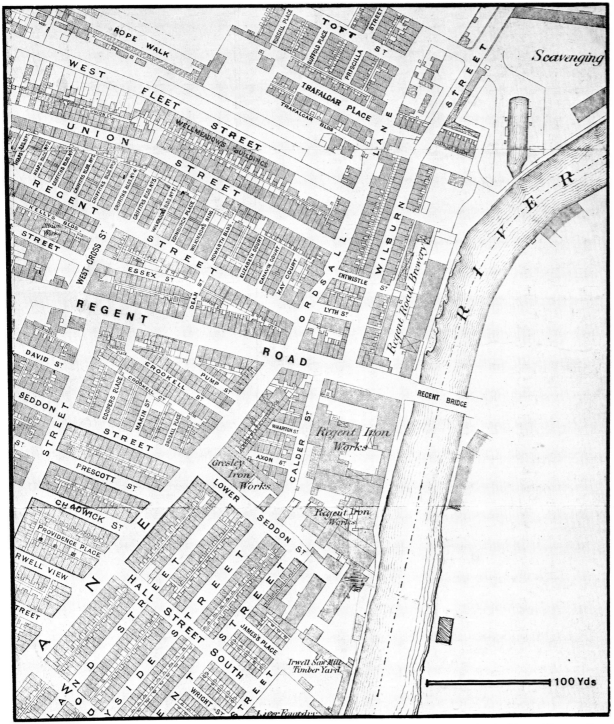

In Ordsall, factories had captured riverside sites but, in contrast to Kersal, it was densely built up in the second half of the nineteenth century with typical Victorian working class houses. The first, immediately behind the larger houses on both sides of Regent Road, were back-to-back dwellings but later development, towards Ordsall Hall, commenced the seemingly endless rows of bye-law property, now being cleared.

BROUGHTON 1820-1970

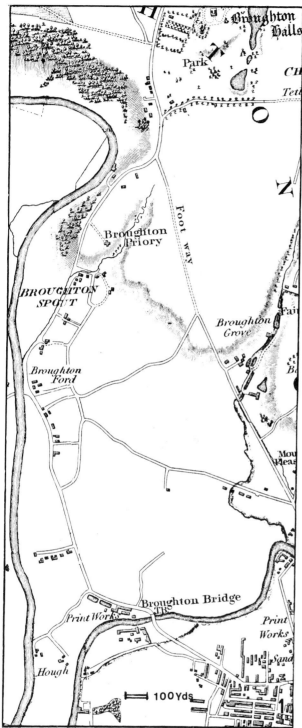

The houses of the original hamlet clustered round the Ford and Broughton Spout but the last 150 years have seen the completely rural field pattern of Lower Broughton change to the overall geometrical grid of suburban housing. This followed the construction of Broughton Bridge, Great Clowes Street, Bury New Road and Broughton Lane with their resultant tramway routes linking the area to the urban centre.

INDEX

76

SOURCES

Acknowledgement is made to the Salford Museum and Art Gallery for illustrations on pages 17 (5), 44 (2), and 69 (3); to Chetham's Library for page 16 (1); Manchester Central Library for pages 13 (4, 5), 20 (4) and 24 (1); the *Salford City Reporter* for pages 26 (1), 52 (5), 59 (2) and 69 (2); Mr Percy Morten for pages 44 (3) and 55 (5) and the Salford City Engineer for page 49 (9). Pages 49 (7) and 50 (3) are reproduced from the Ordnance Survey maps of 1908 and 1922 and page 68 (2) is based on the map of 1848. Permission to use the map on page 74 (2) was given by Geographia Ltd. and to reproduce the photograph on page 68 (4) by *The Guardian*. The remainder of the maps, prints and photographs are from the author's collection and he is indebted to Mr. D. Rendell, of Hale, for making prints from his negatives.